THE FCA

AN ILLUSTRATED HISTORY

THE FCA

AN ILLUSTRATED HISTORY

**DENIS CARROLL, MICHAEL DEEGAN,
STEPHEN KELLY, MARIE HENNESSY & WILLIAM SHEEHAN**

The
History
Press
Ireland▶

To all those who have served

'An FCA member leaving camp brings with them something more than sore feet. They depart with a sense of achievement in that they have voluntarily devoted part of their holidays to the service of their country. Behind them are many hours of rigorous training which they have experienced discipline of a type that is only found in the army and is extremely beneficial in the formation of a strong character.' (Cpl Joe Ahern, *Rockwell College Year Book*)

First published 2011

The History Press Ireland
119 Lower Baggot Street
Dublin 2
Ireland
www.thehistorypress.ie

© Dennis Carroll, Michael Deegan, Marie Hennessy,
Stephen Kelly and William Sheehan, 2011

The right of Dennis Carroll, Michael Deegan, Marie Hennessy,
Stephen Kelly and William Sheehan to be identified as the Authors
of this work has been asserted in accordance with the
Copyrights, Designs and Patents Act 1988.

British Library Cataloguing in Publication Data.
A catalogue record for this book is available from the British Library.

isbn 978 1 84588 718 6

Typesetting and origination by The History Press

CONTENTS

ACKNOWLEDGEMENTS

We would like to thank Lieutenant-Colonel Liam O'Carroll, the Director of Reserve Forces for providing the foreword for this book.

This book would not have been possible without the contributions and efforts of the individuals, both serving and retired, from the units of the FCA between 1946 and 2005. There was a tremendous response to our request for photographs which we hope will act as a reminder to the country of the men and women that have served in the FCA and of the time that they so selflessly gave in the service of the State. We think that it is important to recognise, capture and preserve their efforts in this pictorial history.

We also wish to acknowledge the support of Brigadier-General Paul Packenham, GOC, 1st Southern Brigade, whose help was also critical to the success of the project. Commandant Victor Laing of the Military Archives has also been an invaluable friend and supporter of this project. We would also like to thank Lieutenant Colonel Brendan O'Shea, O/C Sarsfield Barracks and Commandant Connie Whelan, who have supported this project from the beginning. We have had many well wishers including Lieutenant General Noel Bergin (Retd) and Colonel J. O'Sullivan (Retd) and many more to whom we are eternally grateful but are too numerous to mention on an individual basis.

We are eternally grateful to all those who sent us pictures and regret that all of them could not be included in the book. We wish to thank the following: Gerry Mitchell, Peter J. Dooley, Michael Fitzpatrick, Robert Murphy, David Flood, Tony Brady, John Bailey, Gerry Purcell, Peter J. Riordan, Roy O'Hanlon, Paul Burke, Charlie Maye, Dr Louis O'Brien, John Byrne, Tony McNamara, Thomas Cullen, Peter O'Kelly, Patrick T. Sheehan, Ciaran Boyle, Damian Concannon, Philip Dee, Ian Conlan, Robbie Gillan, Noel Molloy and Denis O'Connell. To those who we have not mentioned we also thank very much. We would also like to thank Flight Sergeant Perkins for providing the photographs of the unit flashes.

We would also like to thank our families and friends for their support and patience during the two years this project took.

The photographs that are included here reflect the very diverse nature of the Defence Forces, from the Artillery, Infantry, Cavalry, Signals, Military Police, Engineers, Transport and the Slua Muirí. The photographs also reflect the geographical area of different commands in the East, West, Curragh and the South.

All the images that we have received will be donated with the information from where they came to the Military Archives in Cathal Brugha Barracks Dublin for future researchers and historians to pore over and reflect on the contribution of the servicemen and women of the FCA to the State.

Last, but certainly not least, we would like to thank Ronan Colgan, Beth Amphlett and everyone at The History Press Ireland for all their help and support.

All of the authors' profits will be donated to the Organisation of National Ex-Servicemen and the Sarsfield Barracks Museum.

FOREWORD

The Reserve Defence Force and its predecessors, the Local Defence Force and An Fórsa Cosanta Áitiúil have always held a position of prominence in Irish society and in the history of Ireland's Defence Forces.

Since the foundation of the state, Ireland's Volunteer Reserve Forces have been an ever-present and constant support and its personnel have given distinguished and honourable service to the State.

It is said that 'a picture paints a thousand words' and this excellent production is a testament to that adage. This pictorial overview has captured a collection of unique images of An Fórsa Cosanta Áitiúil throughout the years 1946-2005 and provides the reader with the opportunity to turn back the pages on the illustrious history of the organisation. These rare and nostalgic photographs have now been captured for posterity in this excellent compilation of high quality production.

Well done to all involved in this venture! Great credit must be given primarily to the authors of this work who tirelessly and painstakingly researched and selected these historical images. Thanks and credit must also be given to all of those reservists (past and present) who have contributed material to this excellent production. As a result of your combined efforts future generations of servicemen and women of the reserve will be in a position to view, in a historical perspective, the rich heritage of An Fórsa Cosanta Áitiúil.

Lt Col. Liam O'Carroll
A/Director Reserve Defence Forces

INTRODUCTION

In 1940, while the situation was deteriorating in Europe, the Irish government established a Local Security Force (LSF) to assist An Garda Síochána in its duties. The force was made up of part-time volunteers. The LSF saw its mission change over time and as its numbers grew and some units were tasked with duties which were of a more military nature than policing. As a result of this, the Local Defence Force (LDF) was created in 1941 from units which had previously been part of the LSF It was placed under the control of the Army. It consisted primarily of rifle battalions, which were to supplement the Army in the event of an invasion. The value of such a reserve was proven during the war and in 1946, the Government decided to replace the LDF with a new force, An Fórsa Consanta Áitiúil, the FCA This was to be a volunteer force, composed of ordinary men who would undertake military training in addition to their work and other responsibilities. This of course was not a new concept; the Irish Volunteers had been formed in 1913. We should also remember the many Irishmen who served in the Special Reserve of the British Army and the earlier Militias, and the Irish Volunteers of the eighteenth century to understand the depth of history of part-time military service in Ireland.

The FCA, though under the control and direction of the Department of Defence, was to remain separate from the Irish Army until 1959, when it was integrated into the Army and reorganised so that its structure replicated that of the Army. It was to mirror the Army and new units such as Military Police, Artillery and Engineering companies were established. But as the reader will see, the FCA was firmly rooted in the local, almost like the Pals Battalions of the First World War. We have pictures showing the early units in areas like New Ross, Pallas, and Clonakilty to name but a few. The local FCA was part of the social fabric of every town or village. They were familiar to all from St Patrick's Day parades and Guards of Honour for Presidential visits.

In 1969, with the advent of the Northern Ireland troubles, elements of the FCA were mobilised to assist the Army. FCA personnel deployed with the Army on both border duties, internal security operations and to supplement barrack garrisons. Indeed, many members of the FCA were transferred to full-time service during this period. But at its core in this as in all the other periods of its history was a commitment to training young men and later women in a tradition of national service rooted in the spirit of volunteerism, and in providing them with a military education that would stand to them all their days.

The year 1984 saw yet another change for the FCA as it was restored to the status of a separate organisation within the Defence Forces. The move however did little to alter either the structure or training of the FCA, as it remained a key resource for the Army. A review of the viability and usefulness of a reserve force began in 1996, and when completed in 2000, the need for a reserve was re-affirmed in the Defence White Paper of 2000. A second Defence review in 2002 recommended a return to an integrated force, and on foot of this recommendation, the then Minister Michael Smith agreed that the FCA should be replaced by a Reserve Defence Force (RDF). As a result of this, the FCA was stood down on 1 October 2005, and replaced by the new force, the RDF, many of the serving personnel remained, and while the new organisation is different, it still embodies the volunteer ethos that was at the heart of the old FCA.

This book is a pictorial record to honour an organisation that is now gone and to detail the commitment given by the many who served in it through all the years.

1

THE 1940s

The New Ross LDF, 1943.

KILDANGAN L.D.F. BRANCH 1941

Back row: Mick Brennan. John Byrne. Matt Kelly. Mick Lawless. Pat Casey.
Middle: Liam Quinn. Terry Fitzpatrick. Anthony Larkin. Johnny O'Neill. Ned Murray.
              Jack Murphy.
Front: Willie Shorte. Jackie Aspell. Christy Morgan.

◄ The Kildangan LDF, 1941. The LDF were the Reserve Force prior to the FCA.

▼ 44 Squadron in full cavalry dress.

41 Squadron taking part in a cycle race.

The 11th Cyclist Regiment at Renmore Barracks, 1947.

▲ The Annual Mass Parade of the Belvedere College Company, Pearse Battalion, 1948.

▲ Members of Pallas Battalion relax during the 'S' Command inter-battalion competition.

▲ The New Ross and District
FCA Battalion, 1947.

▶ Members of the North Meath Battalion
provide an altar guard at Clonmellon, Co.
Westmeath, 1948.

◀ FCA Officer Lieutenant Jack Mulcahy receiving his commission.

▼ The first commissioning ceremony for FCA officers at Cathal Burgha Barracks, 1946.

▲ An FCA Guard of Honour from the Pearse Battalion for Archbishop John McQuaid, one of the soldiers is Patrick Cooney who later became Minister of Defence, *c.* 1949.

▲ Battalion officers and NCOs 11th Transport Company, at Cathal Burgha Barracks in 1946.

▲ Members of the Pallas Battalion with competition trophies.

▲ The Pallas Battalion with Bren gun carriers.

2

THE 1950s

▲ Members of the 44th Artillery before a parade in Cork.

◀ Reserve members of the 1st Field Artillery Regiment operate a 4.5-inch howitzer battery.

▶ The 11th Field Signals.

▲ Members of the North Meath Battalion receiving rifle instruction at Gormanstown in 1952.

▲ A Bren Gun Carrier on parade in Cork.

▲ The 11th Motor Squardron man a Beaverette Armoured Car.

▲ Members of the 47th Infantry Battalion outside Blarney in 1953.

CLONAKILTY BATTALION

▲ The Clonakilty members of the 23rd Infantry Battalion at Lynch Camp, Kilworth.

Members of the 48th Infantry Battalion.

Members of the 11th Motor Squadron on a driving course.

DRIVING CLASS
J. Levins, A. Mullarkey, B. Devine

A dodge truck of the 11th Field Signals.

▲ President Sean T. O'Kelly reviews members of the 11th Motor Squadron in Maynooth.

Members of the New Ross Battalion at camp in Gormanstown in 1953.

Members of the 48th Infantry Battalion on parade.

▲ 'A' company of the 48th Infantry Battalion.

▲ The 48th Infantry Battalion at Clancy Barracks.

◀ A company of the 11th Field Engineers.

▶ The 11th Field Engineers waiting for some army food in the Glen of Imaal.

◄ The Slua Mhuirí on parade in Sarsfields Barracks.

➤ The Slua Muirí in winter dress on the range.

▲ The Slua Muirí in a classroom, P Block, Sarsfield Barracks.

▲ The Slua Muirí in a classroom, P Block, Sarsfield Barracks.

▲ A Slua Muirí member training on a naval gun in Sarsfield Barrcks. The gun was rumoured to have come from the Helga.

▲ Newbridge College Company, Pearse Battalion, on parade in 1954.

▲ Tom Barry walks the New Ross Battalion through Crossbarry in 1954.

▲ Tom Barry meets the New Ross Battalion FCA, 1954.

➤ The Boyne area rifle team of the North Meath Battalion in 1955.

◀ 44th/45th Field Artillery Battery shooting team, The Curragh, 1956.

◀ Members of the 11th Motor Squadron train on the Vickers gun at Renmore Barracks in Galway under the instruction of Sergeant Peader Grimes in 1958.

▶ The Rifle team of 'B' Company, 23rd Infantry Battalion, 1958.

▲ The North Louth Battalion, Dundalk, provide a Guard of Honour at An Tostal in 1958.

The funeral parade in Dundalk of Corporal Kevin Duffy who died in service with the FCA in 1958.

◀ Minister of Defence Mr Hilliard inspects the 11th Motor Squadron in 1958.

F.C.A.
CHRISTIAN BROTHERS COLLEGE
CORK.
THE FIRST PLATOON.
Formed 1959.

From rear:- R. Dineen, M. Sheehan, R. Martin, N. Deasy, J. Murphy, W. Moore, D. Buckley, G. Muldowney, M. Howell, R. Cosgrave, R. Kearney, B. Murphy, F. Hayes, R. Dunne, P. Neiland, D. Buckley, T. O'Byrne, R. O'Leary, J. O'Sullivan, J. Ryan, B. Cullen, N. Wallace, A. Foley, T. Brassel, F. McCarthy, T. Launoff, D. Kelleher, P. Gamble, Capt. T.J. Ahern, Capt. D.C. Crowley, Br. D.F. Flannery, Commdt. P. Keogh, Commdt. E. Driver, C. Carroll, R. Byrne, P. Flowey, A. Bennett.

➤ The Christian Brothers College platoon, Cork in 1959.

▲ President Eamonn de Valera inspects a guard of honour from Terenure College in 1959.

▲ Private Eoin O'Sullivan and Tom Sheehan on guard duty at Fort Templebreedy.

➤ The Slua Muirí on a Motor Torpedo Boat.

◄ Loading a Torpedo.

3

THE 1960s

▲ The 11th Field Signals in Clonmel, 1968.

▲ Members of the 8th Infantry Battalion training in tactics.

▶ A funeral firing party for Trooper Butterly, 1961.

◀ The FCA members of the 1st Field Corps of Engineers at Fort Templebreedy.

▲ A reserve 4.5-inch gun crew of the 1st Field Artillery Regiment training in the Glen of Imaal.

▲ 3rd Field Supply and Transport Company at the 1st School of Motoring at Ballymullen Barracks, Tralee, 1960.

◄ Members of the 3rd Field Supply and Transport Company take the Oath of Allegiance, 1960.

► Members of the 8th Infantry Battalion at the Rededication of Kilkerley Catholic church in 1961.

▲ An inspection by the G.O.C of Southern Command of 'B' Company, 23rd Infantry Battalion.

Band members photographed in front of Kilkenny Castle in 1961 or 1962. Drum Major Sam McDonald towers above the others at the back centre. Pipe Major Martin Bradley (the only member still with the band), is at the extreme left of the back row. Photos provided by author.

▲ The New Ross FCA Pipe Band at Kilkenny Castle.

▲ The 11th Field Engineers build a Bailey Bridge on exercise.

▲ The 11th Field Engineers finish a Bailey Bridge.

◀ The 1st Field Artillery Regiment in Ballincollig.

▶ Commandant O'Leary issues uniform to a recruit to the 3rd Field Supply and Transport Company.

A commissioning ceremony of the 23rd Infantry Battalion.

▲ Members of the 23rd Infantry Battalion on a potential NCOs course in Fermoy in 1966.

The 8th Field Artillery Regiment on St Patrick Day Parade, 1964.

▲ Members of the FCA form a Guard of Honour for the 50th anniversary of the Easter Rising in New Ross, 1966.

Units from the FCA take part in the 50th anniversary parade to commemorate the Easter Rising in Dublin, 1966.

Members of the Old IRA and the FCA parade together on the 50th anniversary of the Easter Rising in New Ross, 1966.

◀ The Army, the FCA and the Slua Muirí commemorate the 50th anniversary of the Easter Rising in Limerick, 1966.

▼ A 14th Infantry Battalion guard of honour for Charles J. Haughey at Cloughjordan. (1966).

◄ Sean Lemass attends the 25th Anniversary Mass of the 11th Motor Squadron, 1967.

► An FCA Guard of Honour for the Opening of O'Hanrahan's Bridge in 1967.

▲ A Bishop's Guard of Honour from the 23rd Infantry Battalion.

Sgt. W Quinn instructing on the Engine at Sarsfield Barracks Limerick in 1968.

◄ Members of 3rd Field Supply and Transport Company receive instruction on engines in Sarsfield barracks in 1968.

➤ The 11th Field Engineers complete a wooden bridge.

◄ A typical FCA outdoor camp of the period.

► A Bedford Terrier.

◄ The 11th Field Engineers hard at work.

Lt. P.Stapleton, I/C Gd of Honour.
Solohead. 1969.

➤ A 3rd Field Supply and
Transport guard of honour,
1969.

▲ 2nd Battery, 1st Field Artillery Regiment at the Glen of Imaal.

◀ Lieutenant Tom Sheehan of the 23rd Infantry Battalion on border duty in 1969.

◀ A 120mm mortar.

▼ 2nd Battery, 1st Field Artillery Regiment Gun Crew in action.

▲ Members of the 11th Field Engineers in a three-legged race.

▲ 14th Infantry Battalion members from Tipperay Town win the All Weapons Combined Cup.

▲ 2nd Battery, 1st Field Artillery Regiment at Ballincollig.

▲ Officers and men of the 11th Field Enginners.

4

THE 1970s

▲ Riot Training for 'B' Company, 23rd Infantry Battalion.

▲ The 3rd Field Military Police Company at Kickham Barracks, Clonmel.

▲ The 11th Cavalry Squadron at Cootehill in 1970.

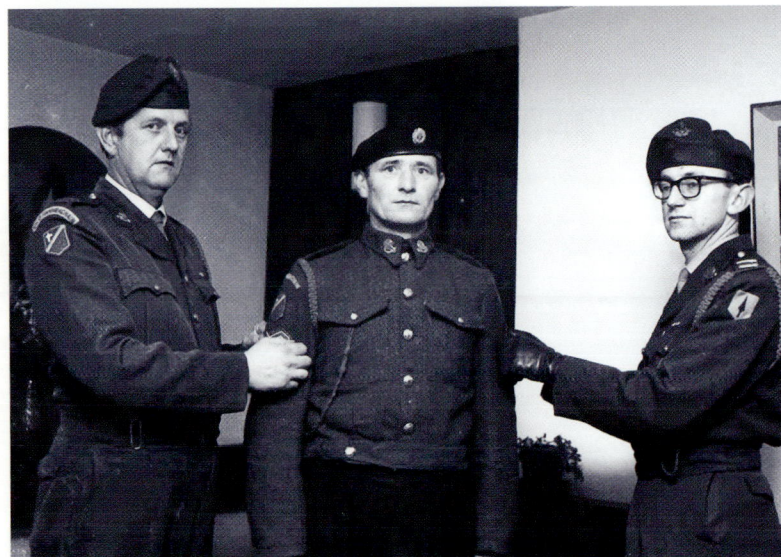

▲ Sgt Flynn gets his stripes from officers of the 10th Infantry Battalion, 1970.

◄ The 7th Infantry Battalion provide an altar guard outside St Colmcille's church in 1973.

▼ A Landsverk armoured car of the 11th Cavalry Squadron, 1972.

◄ Lahinch Camp.

◄ A Ton Class Minesweeper on which Slua Muirí personnel would have served during the 1970s.

➤ A Ton Class Minesweeper on which Slua Muirí personnel would have served during the 1970s.

▲ Members of the 23rd Infantry Battalion with Bren Guns.

▲ Members of the 11th Cavalry Squadron at the Newbridge Festival in 1974.

▲ Sergeant Motherway's reserve gun crew from the 1st Field Artillery Regiment at the Glen of Imaal.

▲ A group of officers from the 11th Field Signals.

▲ Members of the 11th Cavalry Squadron are awarded prizes for best section at Longford in 1977.

▲ The 23rd Infantry Battalion's Gustav team.

▲ Members of the 3rd Field Medical Company who provided support to the 1979 Papal visit to Limerick.

▲ Taoiseach Liam Cosgrave inspects a guard of honour from the 10th Infantry Battalion during an All-Army FCA Shooting Competition at the Curragh, 1977.

5

THE 1980s

▲ Members of the 3rd Anti-Aircraft Battery at Gormanstown.

◄ The 3rd Field Supply and Transport Company training at Donnelly's Hallow in 1982.

► The 3rd Field Supply and Transport Company training at Donnelly's Hallow in 1982.

▲ A member of the 8th Infantry Battalion training with the Bren Gun at Gormanstown.

◄ Corporal L. Shannon receives a presentation on his retirement from officers of the 10th Infantry Battalion in 1981.

► The 3rd Field Supply and Transport Company training in the Burren in 1983.

▲ A St Patrick's Day Colour Party in Limerick, 1985.

▲ The 8th Field Artillery Regiment add some firepower to the *1812 Overture*.

◀ Rockwell College.

▶ A Honour Guard for Bishop
McCormack at Mullingar.

▲ Sgt M. Fitzpatrick of 3rd Anti-Aircraft Battery accepts the All Army prize for the Gustav shoot in 1984.

▲ A gun from the 3rd Anti-Aircraft Battery at Shannon, 1986.

▲ Members of the 3rd Anti-Aircraft Battery train with the Gustav machine gun, 1986.

▲ The 9th Field Artillery Regiment Christmas Dinner.

▲ The 11th Field Signals at Clonmel.

◀ The 23rd Infantry Battalion provides a Guard of Honour for President Hillary during the Cork 800, 1985.

▶ FCA NCOs from the 1st Air Defence Regiment at Gormanstown, 1986.

▲ The 25th Infantry Battalion train in the Slieve Mish Mountains in 1986.

▲ Members of the 23rd Infantry Battalion on the range.

▲ A Guard of Honour from the 8th Infantry Battalion.

◀ Sergeant Joe Brandon of the 9th Field Artillery Regiment fords the River Slaney on tactics.

▲ The 3rd Field Signals Company on camp.

➤ 'B' Company, 23rd Infantry Battalion provide a Guard of Honour, Cork.

▲ A Presidential Guard of Honour for President Hillary from the 23rd Infantry Battalion.

▲ The 14th Infantry Battalion provide a Guard of Honour for President Hillary at Rathkeale.

◄ Officers and Senior NCOs of the 8th Field Artillery Regiment.

▼ The 8th Infantry Battalion on parade.

◀ The first unit shoot of the AML 60, 11th Motor Squadron, 1985.

▼ A 9th Field Artillery Regimental Dinner.

◀ Second Lieutenants Quillivan, O'Donovan and O'Byrne being commissioned at the Curragh, 1986.

▲ The last Landsverk shoot with 20mm Hispano canons by the 11th Motor Squadron.

▲ 'B' Company, 23rd Infantry Battalion take a break on a route march from Kenmare to Killarney.

➤ Training with the Panhards in the Curragh in 1987.

◄ The 3rd Field Military Police Company at Clonmel.

➤ The 9th Field Artillery Regiment provides a Guard of Honour for President Hillary in Sligo, 1989.

◀ 3rd Field Supply and Transport Company Recruit training at Ballymullen, 1989.

▶ ML90 Panhards of the 11th Motor Squadrons in Longford.

◀ The 8th Infantry Battalion on camp.

6

THE 1990s

▲ Members of the 8th Field Artillery Regiment fire a 25 pounder in the Glen of Imaal.

◄ Members of the 22nd Battalion train with an 81mm mortar and 84mm anti-tank weapon.

➤ Adventure training with the 8th Field Artillery Regiment.

▲ 21st Battery, 8th Field Artillery Regiment 120mm mortar crew at the Glen of Imaal.

▲ Members of the 22nd Infantry Battalion on tactics.

▲ Members of the 22nd Infanry Battalion on parade.

▲ The first female recruit platoon, 3rd Field Signals Southern Command at Kilcoran range.

◄ The 3rd Field Supply and Transport Company's Gustav Team.

► A 25 pounder of the 9th Field Artillery Regiment at the Glen of Imaal.

Sgt. T. Jessops Gun Crew 15Th Bty.

▲ Captain Eamonn Mooney of the 7th Infantry Battalion fires the Lee Enfield for the last time, 1992.

▲ Potential NCOs Course with members from the 14th, 22nd, and 23rd Infantry Battalion at Tralee in 1992.

▲ Learning to March, Member of 'A' Company, 23rd Infantry Battalion on the square at Collins Barracks.

◄ The 14th Infantry Battalion in Kilworth in 1996.

➤ Cpl Eddie McInerney and Private Keenan of the 14th Infantry Battalion on tactic in the Glen of Imaal in 1994.

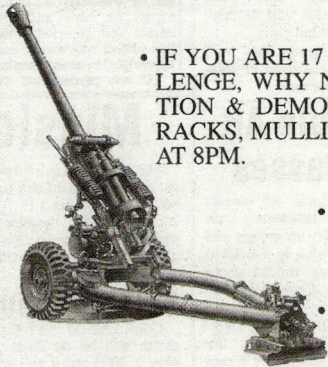

9th Field Artillery Regiment (FCA)

- WE ARE CURRENTLY SEEKING NEW RECRUITS FOR THE RESERVE DEFENCE FORCES.

- IF YOU ARE 17 OR OVER AND SEEKING A NEW CHALLENGE, WHY NOT COME ALONG TO OUR INFORMATION & DEMONSTRATION NIGHT AT COLUMB BARRACKS, MULLINGAR, ON TUESDAY 24TH SEPTEMBER AT 8PM.

- OR TELEPHONE US DURING OFFICE HOURS AT 044 48391 EXT. 1418.

- THE DEFENCE FORCES ARE AN EQUAL OPPORTUNITIES EMPLOYER.

◄ A recruiting advertisement for the 9th Field Artillery Regiment.

➤ Patching up targets in the Butts.

◄ The first female members of the 11th Cavalry Squadron at the Christmas Dinner, 1994.

▲ Heading for the range.

▲ Members of the 14th Infantry Battalion fire the 84mm anti-tank weapon in the Glen of Imaal in 1996.

▲ Cross-country driving, 1995.

▲ A debrief in the field.

◄ The first FCA Quartermasters course for 1st Southern Command personnel at Sarsfield Barracks (including Marie Hennessy, one of the authors).

▲ The 11th Cavalry Squadron on tactics, 1995.

20Th Bty gun crew

◄ A 105mm field gun of the 9th Field Artillery Regiment.

▲ Members of the 23rd Infantry Battalion at Ballymullen Barracks, Tralee.

◀ Members, including the first females, of the 14th Infantry Battalion on camp in Clonmel in 1994.

▶ Members of the 23rd Infantry Battalion arrive at camp for camp at Tralee..

➤ On tactics.

◄ Members of the 9th Field Artillery Regiment on a mortar shoot at the Glen of Imaal in 1992.

➤ Sergeant John O'Sullivan's mortar crew from the 8th Field Artillery Regiment at the Glen of Imaal.

▲ A civic reception for the 50th anniversary of the 10th Infantry Battalion by New Ross UDC, 1998.

▲ Members of the 1st FCA Driving Instructors Course, 1996.

▲ A member of the 23rd Infantry Battalion on tactics.

◀ Members of the 21st Infantry Battalion at the Old Coastguard Station, Dun Laoghaire.

➤ The spirit of volunteerism.

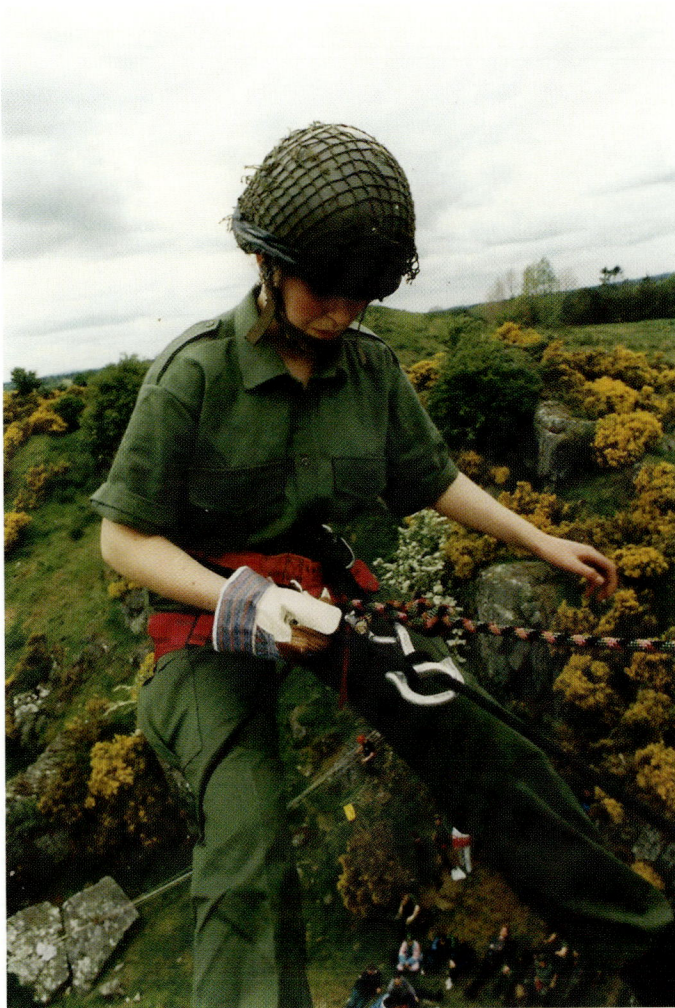

▲ Don't look down! Adventure training with the Engineers.

▲ A Giraffe Radar Station.

An 8th Infantry Battalion Honour Guard.

Casualty evacuation training.

◀ Rifle inspection for members of 22nd Infantry Battalion at Lahinch Camp.

Sgt. J Duffy inspects FN Rifles

▼ Training in foot drill for members of the 23rd Infantry Battalion.

➤ Members of the 3rd Anti-Aircraft Battery man a
0.5-inch Browning machine gun at Farranfore airport,
Co. Kerry in 1998.

▼ Privates MacCionnceannain, Jones, and O'Murchu
of the 20th Infantry Battlion at the Glen of Imaal,
1994.

▲ The 11th Cavalry Squadron motorbike display team, 1998.

◄ A stand-down parade for Commandant Christy Smyth of the 7th Infantry Battalion at Kells, Co. Meath in 1998.

► A decommissioned Landsverk of the 11th Cavalry Squadron being handed over to the Dutch Army for their Armour Museum in 1999.

▲ Members of the 14th Infantry Battalion at Tralee.

7
THE 2000s

▲ Members of the 3rd Field Military Police Company.

◄ A member of the 11th Cavalry Squadron using the Steyr with night sight, 2001.

▼ Members of 22nd Infantry Battalion on the range.

◀ Preparing for a St Patrick's Day Parade, 2002.

➤ Recruit Class, 11th Cavalry Squadron with a Comet Tank in the background in 2004.

◀ Members of the 8th Field Artillery Regiment on morning parade in Mullingar.

◄ Members of the 23rd Infantry Battalion fire the Bren gun.

➤ A member of the 11th Field Signals on the range at Gormanstown.

◄ Members of the 11th Cavalry Squadron present a cheque for £12,500 to Temple Street Children's Hospital, 2001.

➤ Members of the 3rd Anti-Aircraft Battery on parade in Dundalk in 2001.

▲ Members of the 9th Field Artillery Regiment in a tug of war contest.

▲ Members of the 10th Infantry Battalion who helped support the Special Olympics in 2003.

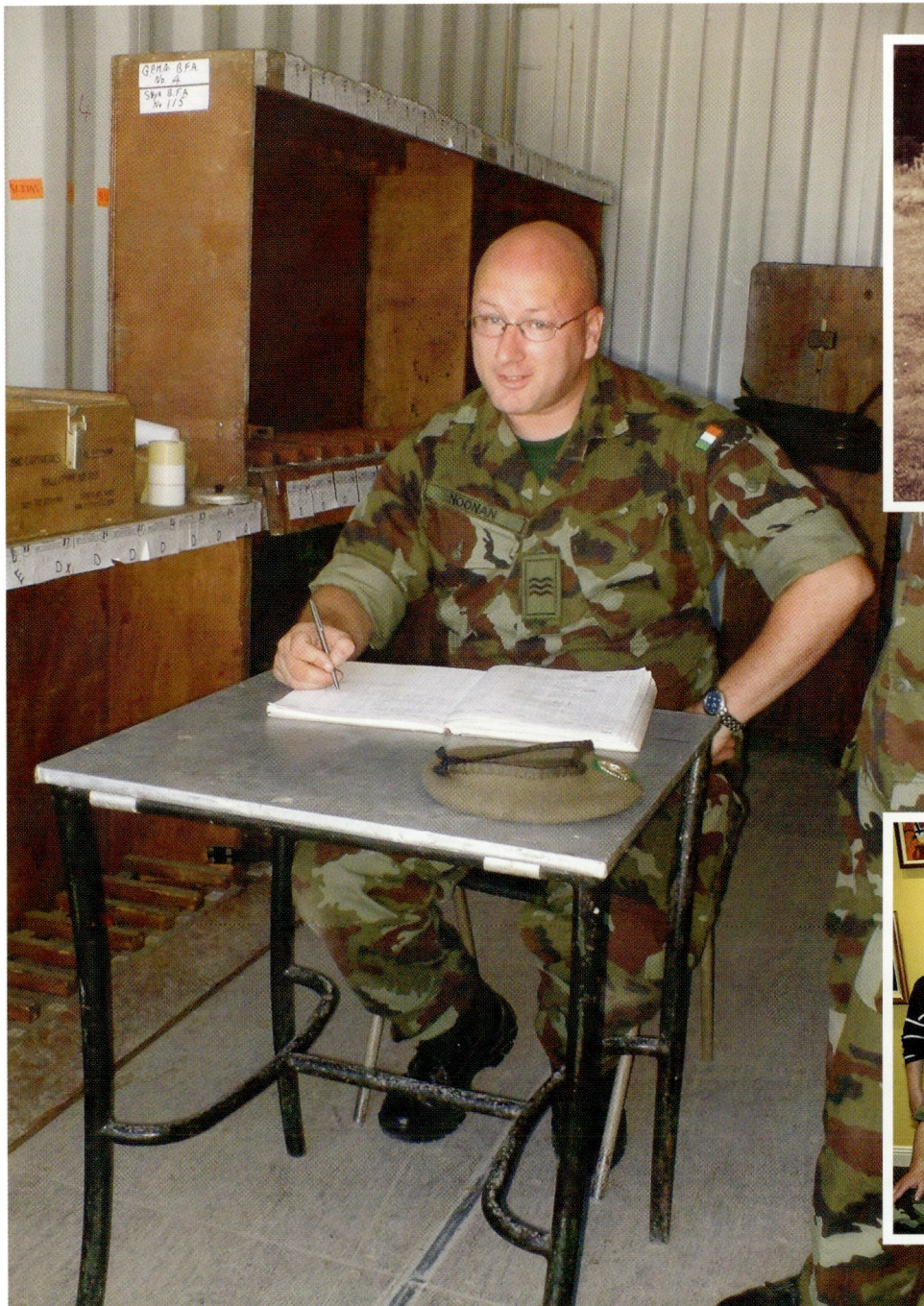

▲ Sgt Noonan issuing stores at Kilworth in 2004.

▲ The 7th Infantry Battalion line the route for the re-internment procession of the ten Irish Volunteers from Mountjoy prison to Glasnevin cemetery, 2003.

▲ Members of 8th Field Artillery Regiment clean their guns.

▲ Members of the 14th Infantry Battalion on camp at Kilworth.

◀ The 8th Field Artillery Regiment at Southern Command's Falling Plate Competition, 2004.

➤ Training in search procedures during an exercise at Kilworth.

▲ Members of 23rd Infantry Battalion prepare for a tactical exercise at Kilworth.

▲ Members of the 23rd Infantry Battalion on exercise at Fort Davis.

▲ Members of the 22nd Infantry Battalion on exercise in Kilworth in 2004.

▲ Members of the 22nd Infantry Battalion on the range.

▲ Members of the 22nd Infantry Battalion on tactics.

► Members of the 23rd Infantry Battalion take part in Exercise New Dawn in 2004.

◄ Members of the 23rd Infantry Battalion take part in Exercise New Dawn in 2004.

◄ 7th Battalion on tactics.

▼ The 9th Field Artillery Regiment hold an open air mass at the Glen of Imaal.

◄ 7th Battalion under attack.

▲ On tactics in Kilworth in 2004.

▲ The 8th Field Artillery Regiment training at the Glen of Imaal in 2005.

▲ The stand-down party of the 8th Field Artillery Regiment at Collins Barracks, 2005.

APPENDIX

Regional Command and Command HQ Flashes

Artillary Unit Flashes

Engineers Unit Flashes

Cavalry Unit Flashes

Infantry Unit Flashes

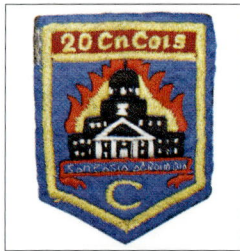

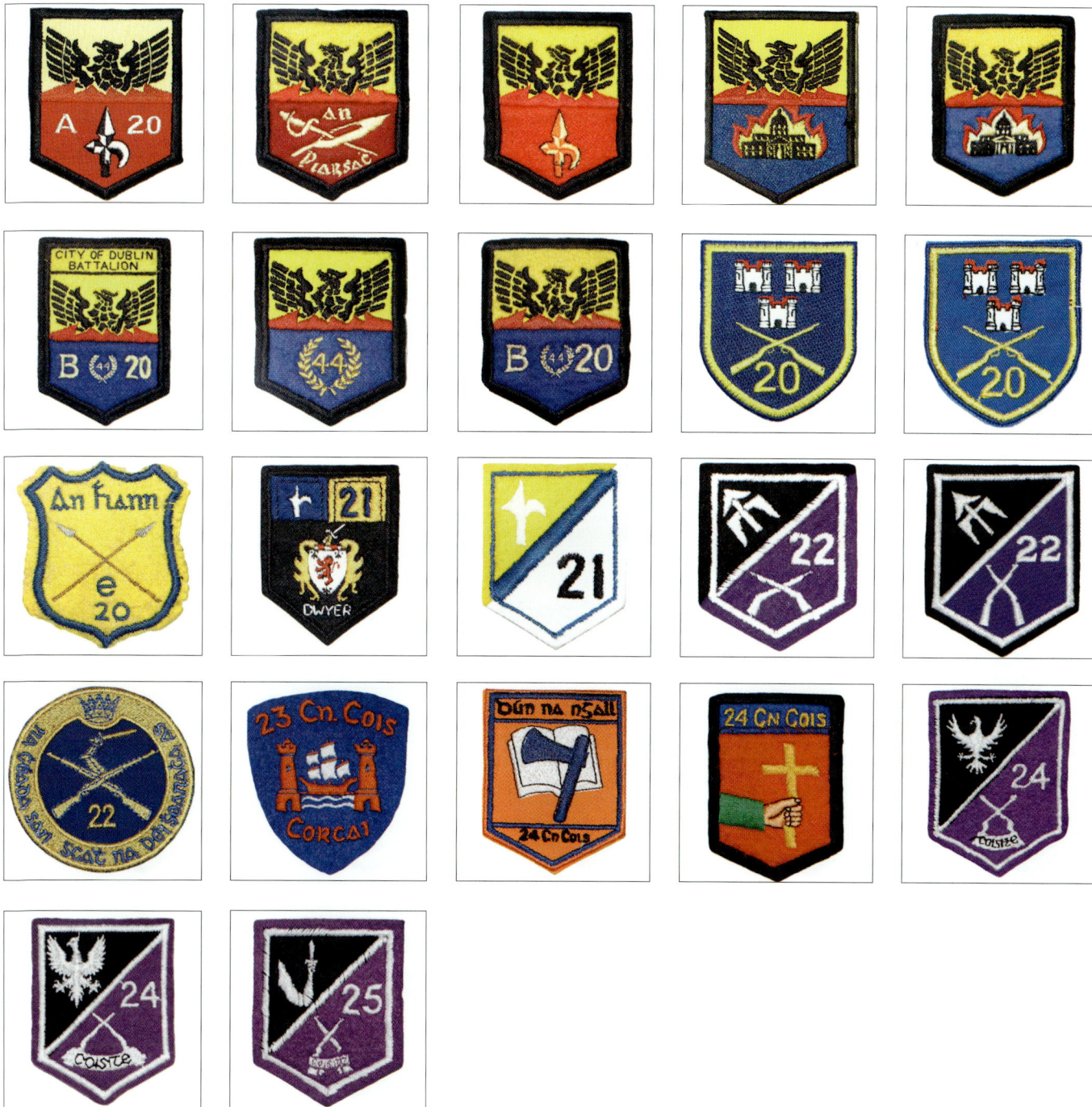

ABOUT THE AUTHORS

Sergeant Michael Deegan served with the 3rd Anti-Aircraft Battery as a reservist and joined the Irish Defence Forces in 1985. He served with the 12th Infantry Battalion until 2007 and is currently serving as PDF Cadre with the 31st Reserve Logistical Support Battalion in Sarsfield Barracks. He has a degree in Geography and History and a Masters' Degree in History. He was a co-author of *Images of Sarsfield Barracks* with Denis Carroll, Stephen Kelly and William Sheehan. He has served overseas five times: in Lebanon twice, Yugoslavia, Kosovo and Chad.

Private Denis Carroll (Rtd) has had a long interest in military history. He joined the 3rd Field Signal Company in the late 1960s and served for seven years. He enlisted in the Irish Naval Service in 1978, before transferring to the Army after four years. He served in the 12th Battalion, retiring in March 2009 after thirty-one years' service. Denis was a co-author of *Images of Sarsfield Barracks*.

Sergeant Marie Hennessy-Quaid serves in the 31st Reserve Logistical Support Battalion's Transport Company previously 3rd Field Supply and Transport Company. She is coming up the her twentieth year of membership with the Reserve Defence Force and has the privilege to say that she was one of the first females into the FCA. Marie has a keen interest in local history and is a member of her local history society. She is a member of the National Executive of the Reserve Defence Forces Representative Association (RDFRA).

A/CQMS Stephen Kelly currently serves as a member of the PDF Cadre with the 31st Reserve Military Police Company in Sarsfield Barracks Limerick. He has previously served with D Company 8th Infantry Battalion FCA, 2nd Field Artillery Regiment, 29th Infantry Battalion, 2nd Garrison Military Police Coy, 3rd Garrison Military Police Coy and the 1st Southern Brigade Military Police Company. In addition, A/CQMS Kelly has served over seas in Lebanon with Military Police Section 63rd Battalion and 89th Battalion UNIFIL. He established the Military Museum in Sarsfield Barracks, Limerick and is currently its curator. A/CQMS Kelly was also a co-author of *Images of Sarsfield Barracks*.

Dr William Sheehan is a lecturer and military historian; he served in the 14th and 32nd Infantry Battalions, and the 31st Reserve Military Police Company. He is the author of *British Voices from the Irish War of Independence* and *A Hard Local War: The British Army and the Guerrilla War in Cork, 1919-1921*. He was a co-author of *Images of Sarsfield Barracks*.

FCA medals.